BY SARAH BESSEY

Field Notes for the Wilderness
Field Notes for the Wilderness: A Guided Journal
A Rhythm of Prayer (editor)
Miracles and Other Reasonable Things
Out of Sorts: Making Peace with an Evolving Faith
Jesus Feminist

FIELD NOTES
FOR THE
WILDERNESS:
A GUIDED JOURNAL

FIELD NOTES
FOR THE
WILDERNESS:
A GUIDED JOURNAL

Practices for an Evolving Faith

SARAH BESSEY

CONVERGENT

NEW YORK

A Convergent Trade Paperback Original

Copyright © 2024 by Sarah Bessey

All rights reserved.

Published in the United States by Convergent Books,
an imprint of Random House, a division of
Penguin Random House LLC, New York.

CONVERGENT BOOKS is a registered trademark and the
Convergent colophon is a trademark of
Penguin Random House LLC.

ISBN 9780593593707
Ebook ISBN 9780593593714

Printed in the United States of America on acid-free paper

convergentbooks.com

9 8 7 6 5 4 3 2 1

First Edition

Book design by Diane Hobbing

This path through the wilderness was created by

....

....

....

Date...

Above all, trust in the slow work of God.

—*Pierre Teilhard de Chardin*

CONTENTS

FIELD NOTES
FOR THE
WILDERNESS:
A GUIDED JOURNAL

INTRODUCTION

Dear Friend,

I'm so glad you've decided to embark on this evolving faith journey with intention, thoughtfulness, and reflection. It takes a lot of courage to fully meet ourselves and God in the wilderness. I bless you in this beginning.

Sometimes when we find ourselves in a faith shift, we long to return to who we were before. We miss the black-and-white thinking and the if-this-then-that bargains. We miss the illusion of control and certainty. So initially we look around for a guide or a teacher or someone to *just tell us what to do*. We want the steps, the formula, the way to resolve this discomfort and disorientation quickly in a satisfactory manner.

And yet that's the very thing being untangled in us. All the mediators, scripts, and formulas are gone now. I'm sorry and you're welcome.

In these pages, you are given room to explore and create your own map for the wilderness. It will look different from what I've discovered. I'm genuinely excited for you to begin to craft a vision for yourself, to honor your hopes for what is ahead, and to articulate that longing in cooperation with grace. It's well and good for me to share about my own practices of an evolving faith, but they were all born out of my own experiences, study, relationships, communities, history, and life. Yours may, and likely will, differ. These pages will give you the space to recontextualize those practices for your own life.

In these pages, you'll have the opportunity to think deeply about your own journey. We need intentional space for our own stories. Too often, we've allowed the journeys of others to guide our particular faith formation, having been trained to treat someone else's life as a blueprint for our own. Here, in the pages ahead, your own story will be told. Your unique perspective and social location won't be pushed to the side. Your own priorities will be explored. Here your life is honored, your path forward is created.

SOMETIMES, WHEN I MEET A reader in person, they will ask me to sign their copy of a book I wrote. When they pull out their dog-eared and underlined copy, they often apologize for the state of the pages, which always makes me laugh. That is what I want! To me, there is nothing better than seeing a waterlogged book that fell into the bathtub because you kept reading even after the water cooled off, or seeing crumbs from your lunch on the pages, or sticky notes to remember pages, or crayon scribbles from your kids. I love these things with my whole heart. (For the record: I also read that way. A pen in my hand to mark up pages or write notes in the margins, or dog-earing pages I know I'll revisit, all of it. My books bear the mark of me and our then-tinies, too.)

So I want to give you permission to just *destroy* this book. Write, doodle, dog-ear, color-code pages, make your mark. Your story matters and these pages will stand as a testimony to this moment in your life. Years from now, when you stumble across this book on a shelf, you'll crack it open to the notes in the margins and the stories you told and the reflections you wrote. And you'll love this version of you all over again, even if you make yourself laugh or groan sometimes. Take the time to be honest, courageous, and tell your story as it stands right now. Love the version of you that is still becoming.

Love, S.
Ordinary Time 2023

HOW TO USE THIS GUIDED JOURNAL

I've loosely followed the trajectory of the book so that you can journal as you read. But don't feel bound to that correspondence either; there isn't one right way to wrestle with your own story here.

Answer each of the prompts in a way that feels right for you. Whether that's by listing things in bullet-point format or in poetry, a sketch or a one-sentence response per question or long-form paragraphs, I promise there isn't a wrong way to respond.

You're also welcome to work through these prompts in conversation with a friend or a small group. Not all of us find journaling helpful or a natural experience, but don't let that stop you from trying to find a way to integrate the insights and practices of the book into your own life. Conversation, contemplation, prayer, small group discussions, all of it works. And as I cover in the book, it's good to travel this path with a qualified companion as well, such as a therapist or a spiritual director, perhaps. Asking for real help is wise, so if some of these prompts lend themselves to these kinds of conversations, have at it.

YOU'LL COME ACROSS BREATH PRAYERS within these pages, too. Breath prayer remains an integral part of my own spiritual practice because it hits on something to do with embodiment and quiet that I sorely need in my life. I've found that this form of prayer is an easy point of entry for those of us who sometimes feel a bit weird about prayer in general or have lost the old pathways. Sometimes this is the only way I can pray for broad stretches of time. It makes some kind of connection between my body and my soul, and deep breaths are never bad for any of us.

In case you haven't encountered breath prayer before, it is an ancient form of contemplation and it is easily adaptable. Simply choose one or two lines to meditate on while you inhale and then exhale slowly. You can pray a breath prayer literally anywhere without special rituals or space or intention.

I've found that I like to be in a quiet corner for a few minutes, and I usually start by lighting a candle. When you've found a place that works for you and made it prayerful for yourself, I suggest just gently becoming aware of your body. Sit in a way that is comfortable for you, a position that will allow you to take deep breaths in and out. Close your eyes. Imagine a room or a place where you feel safe, as your own sanctuary. It can be a real physical space from your own life or history or one that exists in your imagination. Picture yourself in that sanctuary. Imagine the way the air smells and the way the light feels. Breathe slowly and deeply while holding that place in your mind for a few moments, until you have all the details of it gathered around your soul. You'll enter into your time of prayer or meditation from within that sanctuary.

THE MOST COMMON OR HISTORIC form of breath prayer is known as the Jesus Prayer. So, with that as an example, here's how it works:

Inhale

Fill your whole self with breath.
Feel the air in your lungs.
And then pray:
"Lord Jesus Christ, son of God,"

Exhale

Slowly and fully,
conclude with the rest of the prayer:
"Have mercy on me, a sinner."

And simply repeat this practice. Start with five good breaths in and out, with the words spoken aloud or quietly held in your mind; it's up to you. That's it, really. Whenever you come across a breath prayer in this journal, you can pause right in that moment to breathe through the invitation on the page or you can come back to it later.

MAY YOU MEET YOUR OWN story with grace, my friend.

May you take these moments of reflection to honor where you have been and prepare for the road ahead.

May you encounter the goodness and hope of God in ways that surprise you.

And may you always know that you are loved.

May you receive losing your religion like the gift it will be to you in the end.

The wilderness isn't a problem to be solved, it is another altar of intimacy with God.

What did the metaphorical "city" look like or feel like for you? Did you ever belong in the city?

....
....
....
....
....
....
....

Describe your spiritual upbringing. What key moments or milestones can you point to as markers? What were the moments of joy and the moments of pain?

....
....
....
....
....
....
....

What caused you to cross the threshold to the wilderness?

....
....
....
....
....
....

What were the factors that compelled you to turn your face away from the certainty of the city?

....

....

....

....

....

....

When was the last time God surprised you? Describe that experience.

....

....

....

....

....

....

In the book there's a story about finding an unexpected stream in the middle of the desert and how it allowed Sarah to see the grace of God. Write about an experience with a "stream in the desert," a moment when you received unexpected confirmation and grace and sustenance.

....

....

....

....

....

How have you understood—or misunderstood—deconstruction in the past? How does your community or context currently speak of the experience?

....
....
....
....
....
....
....
....
....
....
....
....
....
....
....
....
....
....

How would you describe the idea of deconstruction to someone who has never heard of it before?

....
....
....
....
....
....

What was something you misunderstood about deconstruction before experiencing it for yourself?

....

....

....

....

....

....

....

❧

Breath Prayer

Inhale: *I bless my own unknowing,*
Exhale: *I invite the Spirit to this path of becoming.*

❧

What do you think about the term "evolving faith"? Is there another word or phrase that resonates for you instead?

....

....

....

....

....

....

....

An evolving faith brings new ideas and ancient paths together. It's about rebuilding and reimagining a faith that works not only for ourselves but for the whole messy, wide, beautiful world. . . . An evolving faith is a resilient and stubborn form of faithfulness that is well acquainted with the presence of God in our loneliest places and deepest questions. And an evolving faith has room for all the paths you may navigate after our time together in these pages.

We find ourselves in the wilderness for many different reasons. Sometimes the final push over the threshold is a big, looming situation that wallops us into a new reality, but it can also be a constellation of smaller reasons and a slower realization. Which of the scenarios or reasons that were named connected with you? Which ones surprised you? Which of your own experiences were missing and need to be named?

God, you're courageous.
And you aren't alone.

What words describe your religious upbringing?

Who or what were the influences on your spiritual formation?

I'm not afraid for you.
If you're honestly seeking God,
I believe you will find what
you're looking for, even if it looks
different than what
I have found.

What were you trained to believe about a life of faith?

Are you surprised that you have landed here in the wilderness? Why or why not?

The first thing we need to learn in the wilderness is generous gentleness.

What does "generous gentleness" look like for you?

"*Are you tired? Worn out? Burned out on religion? Come to me. Get away with me and you'll recover your life. I'll show you how to take a real rest. Walk with me and work with me— watch how I do it. Learn the unforced rhythms of grace. I won't lay anything heavy or ill-fitting on you. Keep company with me and you'll learn to live freely and lightly.*"
—*Matthew 11:28–30, MSG*

Which of the three invitations from Jesus in this passage in Matthew resonates most with you?

1. Do you need the acknowledgment of your burden?

....

....

2. The invitation to come away?

....

....

3. The invitation to learning to live freely and lightly?

....

....

Write a letter to a younger version of yourself, the "you" who was full of certainty and answers or perhaps the "you" who had questions and doubts that you were never able to name. What would you tell them?

....

....

....

....

....

....

....

....

....

....

Breath Prayer

Inhale: *I want to recover my real self.*
Exhale: *Jesus, show me an unforced rhythm of grace.*

Chapter 2

AN EVOLVING
FAITH IS ANOTHER
WAY THROUGH

Describe a time when you lost your old faith pathways altogether and knew that you were going to have to chart a new path.

Are you more likely to "double down" or to "burn it down"?

What does doubling down look like for you? What about burning it down?

If that was your experience, what are some of the doubts, questions, experiences, or aspects of yourself that you stuffed away and hid during a season of "doubling down"?

....

....

....

....

....

What would it look like to welcome and honor those doubts, questions, experiences, or aspects of yourself now?

....

....

....

....

The gap between our ideals and our lived realities can break our hearts. Write about a time when that gap became very pronounced or tangible for you.

....

....

....

How does it feel to think of faith as a cycle rather than a linear path?

....

....

....

Let God meet you in the particular goodness of you, not a printer copy of someone else's best-case scenario for your life.

In Brian McLaren's four stages of faith formation—Simplicity, Complexity, Perplexity, and Harmony—which stage describes your faith journey right now? If you've cycled through the stages a few times, can you find a way to speak lovingly to those versions of yourself?

....
....
....
....
....
....

What have the stages of faith formation taught you about yourself? About your communities? About God?

....
....
....
....
....
....

❧

Breath Prayer

Inhale: *Friend of my soul,*
Exhale: *come journey with me.*

❧

Even as we wander, we're carrying with us, tucked right into the corner of our yearnings, the truth that the love of God is more healing, more lovely, more alive than we imagine.

Chapter 3

MAKE YOUR PEACE WITH THIS TRUTH: YOU WILL CHANGE

*Now is the time
for patience and kindness,
even toward yourself.*

What are you afraid of because of this evolving faith?

Describe the vision of God you were given or concocted. What is false and what is true about that version of God?

Why are you afraid of those things? What is the invitation in your fears?

5

Chapter 5

CULTIVATE HOPE
ON PURPOSE

What do you hope is true about God?

....
....
....
....
....
....
....
....

What does the love of God look like or feel like for you right now?

....
....
....
....
....
....
....
....
....
....
....
....
....
....
....
....

Describe a time when you experienced the love of God. What did that feel like? What do you remember about that experience?

Here in the wilderness Love will look different than you were taught, it will be tougher and stronger and more stubborn.

What does thwarted hope and disappointment feel like in your body?

What are you afraid will happen if you admit to disappointment with God?

In what ways have you been disappointed? What are five of your disappointments that need to be named?

Sometimes our expectations need to be disappointed in order to make room for the true, wise, good Gospel to disrupt us.

What are the expectations you're glad didn't turn out the way you wanted?

_____

_____

_____

_____

_____

_____

_____

_____

_____

What are the things you once believed about God that you're relieved to have released now?

_____

_____

_____

_____

_____

_____

_____

_____

_____

_____

_____

_____

_____

———————

You've had your certainties blown to hell, and it turned out that God was the One who lit the match.

———————

What does it mean for you to cultivate hope in your life right now?

....

....

....

....

....

....

....

....

....

....

....

Describe what hope inspires you to do in your life right now. What work and transformation can you track back to your dogged hopefulness?

....

....

....

....

....

....

....

....

....

....

....

....

....

....

———————

*Your hope—your hope in the
goodness and welcome and love
of God, you wonderful, stubborn
thing—will not disappoint you.*

———————

Breath Prayer

Inhale: *I will cultivate hope in my life,*
Exhale: *and find the holy possibilities in disappointment.*

If you've felt like you had to earn God's love, what would it look like for you to stop striving to earn the love of God?

I trust God's love more than my own fear and more than other people's panic over my soul.

How do you respond when you consider trusting God's love more than your fear or the fear of others?

....

....

....

....

....

....

....

....

....

....

....

....

....

....

....

....

....

....

ะัะ

Breath Prayer

Inhale: *Give me an imagination for our belovedness.*
Exhale: *You are the Love that holds everything together, even me.*

ะัะ

The wilderness is home to God,

even the wilderness inside you.

Chapter 6

TELL THE
TRUTH AND LEARN
TO LAMENT

If we don't deal with our trauma or our sadness or our anger, it begins to deal with us.

The stages of grief—denial, anger, bargaining, depression, acceptance—aren't a linear path. Which stages can you recognize in your own journey? What can you learn about yourself in that stage of grief? What can you learn about God?

Finding meaning can happen after loss. What does finding meaning look like for you right now?

Share about a ritual that has held meaning for you in the past.

Consider a loss you've experienced that could be mourned through ritual. What would that look like?

Name the people who could help you create a ritual to process your losses and truth or to bear witness with you.

What you think is the right and faithful response could actually be the thing tearing you apart from the inside. Until you learn to stop spiritually bypassing your actual life, you won't find meaning, let alone healing.

Share an experience of spiritual bypassing. How did that make you feel? Rewrite that scenario with the imagination of fully embracing lament and grief. What changes?

....

....

....

....

....

....

....

....

....

....

....

....

....

....

....

....

....

....

....

....

....

....

....

....

....

....

....

In a world—and particularly a subculture like evangelicalism— that can run on mutually-agreed-upon half-truths and outright lies, telling the truth is always going to be a prophetic act.

It is good and necessary to ask for and seek out help. List five ways you can reach out for help to process your losses and grief.

The God of overcomers and victors is also in the gutters with those of us whose hearts have been broken.

Write a blessing for something you haven't considered possible to bless.

It's a form of soul care to embody the hope that God is with us, still, in the heartbreak of our lives, too.

What has been your experience with corporate or communal lament? Where have you seen or experienced it in your life, whether that is in church or in your community or elsewhere? How did it help or minister to you?

Write a vision for your own healing. What does "healed" mean to you in that context?

....
....
....
....
....
....
....
....
....
....
....
....
....
....
....
....

❧

Breath Prayer

Inhale: *I will speak the truth,*
Exhale: *and encounter goodness in honesty.*

❧

———————

What was meant to shame you or silence you or punish you will become the making of you.

———————

7

Chapter 7

NOTICE YOUR OWN
SACRAMENTAL LIFE

When was the last time you said "wow"? Describe what was happening and why you responded with awe.

In the book, Sarah tells a story about the kids on the back deck noticing the stars and the wonder of the moment. Describe a "holy interruption" you've experienced recently, a moment when your spirit said, "You're going to want to notice this."

We live into the darkness until it becomes a friend.

Life is often very busy and overwhelming. What would need to happen in your life for you to develop a practice of holy noticing right now?

Steer into the things that leave you asking questions instead of memorizing answers.

Share five things that spark curiosity and wonder in you. Describe how they sustain you in difficult times.

Write a permission slip for your own sense of curiosity, wonder, and unknowing.

Write the ways you are noticing God's unexpected nearness right now.

....

....

....

....

....

....

What is a piece of art that has brought you to tears or evoked a strong emotion in you? It can be a song, a painting, a play, a book, a movie, anything. Why did it prompt such a response from you?

....

....

....

....

....

....

....

....

....

❧

Breath Prayer

Inhale: *I cultivate my awareness of love and beauty.*
Exhale: *The presence of God is all around me.*

❧

I see the sanctuaries and altars and invitations of this place, these people, this moment, and I won't miss it.

8

Chapter 8

GO SLOWLY
ON PURPOSE

What are some theological ideas, concepts, or questions that you want to slowly investigate?

9

Chapter 9

RECLAIM
REPENTANCE

Healing doesn't come because we're so good at faking fine.

How does the word "sin" feel to you now? Did you have a previous connection to the word? Is there a way to reclaim it or do you need to release it?

What has been your personal story with the ideas of repentance and forgiveness, sin and confession?

What does the word "repentance" stir up in you now?

*Repentance is actually a
beautiful, life-giving
reorientation toward God's
good path of flourishing with
ourselves, our neighbors,
and our world.*

Describe a time in your life when you experienced "metanoia"—that changing of a mind that leads to the changing of a life. What happened?

*Repentance is turning back
toward that path of Love.*

It's difficult but necessary to reckon with our failures and wrongdoings. Take a few moments to write out your own confession and repentance. What does atonement look like in this situation? What will change in your life now?

Describe what "quieting your conscience" and "opening your grief" mean for you now. What do you do? Say? Practice?

What is something you need to confess?

❧

Breath Prayer

Inhale: I confess _____,
Exhale: and I turn back toward the path of Love.

❧

Write what you will be doing differently now, on the other side of that confession.

_____

_____

_____

_____

_____

_____

_____

_____

_____

_____

_____

_____

_____

_____

_____

_____

_____

_____

_____

_____

Chapter 10

LEARN TO LOVE
THE WORLD AGAIN

*Wherever this path leads you,
you'll be grateful for all the little
campfires of belonging you found
along the way, all the moments
of hope you cherished, the brief
flickers of love that caught and
in the end, became the hearth of
your life, warming you right
through.*

Write out ten things you know God loves in this world.

What were you taught about loving the world?

Loving is a worthwhile risk, a shot in the dark that illuminates everything, a radical act of faith and hope.

What are ten particular things you love about this world? Be specific.

....

....

....

....

....

....

....

....

....

If love became your motivation for activism and peacemaking in the world, what would shift in your posture and practice?

....

....

....

....

....

....

❧

Breath Prayer

Inhale: *God, you so loved the world.*
Exhale: *Teach me how to love the world, too.*

❧

―――――――

Love this moment of particular grace, not in spite of all the grief and loss surrounding us but because of it.

―――――――

Chapter 11

NURTURE YOUR OWN BELONGING

Describe your experiences with church over your lifetime.

Name the places—religious or otherwise—where you've experienced and found belonging in your life.

If a place of belonging eventually became a source of alienation for you, what happened? What changed? How did that experience affect you?

If you have a friend who has evolved with you or made room for your transformations, write them a letter of gratitude and honor here. Consider sharing it with them.

We're called to embody God's redemptive goodness in the world, together.

Did you grow up in an individual culture or a communal culture? What did you learn from that experience?

....

....

....

....

....

....

....

....

....

....

....

....

....

How does healthy interdependence look for you? What support do you need and what support can you offer to others?

....

....

....

....

....

....

....

....

....

....

....

Do you crave a "congregation" or a community? What scares you about that idea? What draws you to it?

Write five ways that you could begin to expand your notion of belonging. Where are the places you could explore more community interdependence?

No one gets to take Jesus away from you and no one gets to disqualify you from the Church.

Who are the people you trust in your community? Who makes you feel like you belong?

How could you create a sense of belonging for others? Who are the people that are drawn to you right now?

———————

*B*elonging won't require you to become less of yourself. True belonging celebrates the fullness of who you are, all of it.

———————

Describe the last time you experienced belonging. Where are you experiencing belonging right now?

The one guarantee about community is that you will be disappointed at times. What do you plan to do with your disappointment when it inevitably comes around again?

If you feel lonely, create a plan to explore the possibility of finding community again. It doesn't have to be in formal institutional religion; consider alternatives.

⁂

Breath Prayer

Inhale: I deserve love and community.
Exhale: I can cultivate my own belonging.

⁂

You're part of a vast company out here in the wilderness, a whole expanse of people who haven't fit and don't fit.

Chapter 12

LOOK FOR GOOD
TEACHERS

Discernment of good fruit is something you're going to have to learn out here, especially if you've spent a lifetime denying your own intuition and inner knowing in the service of someone else's idea of the greater good.

What is some of the "bad fruit" that you were mistakenly told was good fruit? What impact did that misrepresentation have on your life or the lives of others?

_____

_____

_____

_____

_____

_____

_____

_____

_____

_____

_____

_____

_____

_____

_____

_____

_____

_____

_____

_____

_____

_____

Look for what is bringing life and flourishing into the world.

What is your relationship with your own sense of discernment? Do you feel able to discern what is good fruit versus bad fruit now? What would help you become better acquainted with your own discernment?

Where are you experiencing life and flourishing right now? Where is the good fruit?

We can't do good discernment work without overflowing love right alongside that knowledge and insight.

Describe an experience of reorientation you have had, a time when you realized the story you had been told wasn't true or the full story. What did you learn? How did that experience change you?

Look at your bookshelves, your podcasts, your music, your teachers, your understanding of history. What story is being told there? Whose perspective is missing?

If you've been formed by only one particular voice or experience or social location, then you're missing so much of what makes God beautiful and true, good and loving.

Think of someone who has a story different from your own. What have you learned about loving God and people because of your relationship with that person? How has that experience changed you?

Beyond reading books or listening to podcasts, what are some practical and embodied ways to learn from wise teachers?

Who are some of the greatest theologians you've known, apart from the usual structures of influence and power? Who are the people in your life who have taught you about loving God and loving people well? What did you learn from them?

Write a letter to someone who has been a good teacher on your journey. You can keep it here just for yourself, of course, but consider sending the letter to them so they are aware of their impact on your life.

....
....
....
....
....
....
....
....
....
....
....
....
....
....
....
....
....
....
....

❧

Breath Prayer

Inhale: *I open my heart up to stories that aren't my own.*
Exhale: *I receive disruption as a holy gift.*

❧

Listen, listen, to the many voices

singing God's goodness

that we've silenced and

ignored for too long. There is a

whole choir out here.

13

Chapter 13

BECOME A
NEW EXPLORER
ON AN
ANCIENT PATH

This chapter opens with the story of Sarah paring down her household before her family moved to a new province. List some of the items that you treasure in your home. Tell the story of why each matters to you.

1.

2.

3.

4.

5.

6.

7.

8.

9.

10.

I believe there is room in our homes—and in our lives—for more than just the useful or functional: there is room for the lovely, the memory-filled, the beautiful, the sacred, the just-because-I-love-it-still stuff.

What are the beliefs and practices you need to keep? Toss? Repurpose?

Take a spiritual inventory:

KEEP	TOSS	REPURPOSE

*There is room to honor
and hold space for the precious
and the meaningful even as we
evolve in our beliefs, our homes,
and our lives.*

What is something from your past that you've been surprised to discover is precious to you still?

....

....

....

....

....

....

....

....

What is something you're relieved to throw away?

....

....

....

....

....

....

What is something from the ancient or past versions of Christianity that you think is worth preserving?

....

....

....

....

....

....

....

————————

There is room for our traditions or practices, beliefs or spiritual disciplines to evolve with us.

————————

What is something you'd love to repurpose or reimagine for the future?

How were you taught to pray?

How are you experiencing prayer these days?

You don't have to make fun of everything you used to love, and you certainly don't need to despise it. Handle your old ways with gentleness; you might find something to love here eventually.

What is a form of faithfulness that you've found inspiring? Is there something outside of your own tradition that you would like to explore?

....
....
....
....
....
....
....
....
....
....
....
....
....
....
....
....
....
....
....

⁊

Breath Prayer

Inhale: *I discern good teachers and good fruit.*
Exhale: *I can trust myself.*

⁊

14

Chapter 14

REMEMBER TO BE FOR, NOT JUST AGAINST

Have you ever experienced that feeling Elizabeth Gilbert named as "not this"? Describe the moment.

....

....

....

....

....

....

....

....

....

....

....

....

....

....

....

....

What was the outcome of your own moment of "not this"?

....

....

....

....

....

....

....

....

....

Name your own Against realizations. What are you Against right now? Do you remember the origin of that knowing?

Example:

Against: burnout glorification
    Origin: the week I worked 50+ hours and then got sick

Against: ....

    Origin: ....

....

Against: ....

    Origin: ....

....

Against: ....

    Origin: ....

....

Don't forget to dream of what could be possible. And don't forget to live into that with faithfulness.

What are you For right now? Name your own For realizations.

Consider the rhythm of turning away and turning toward. When you look back at your list of Against, what would you turn toward instead?

TURNING AWAY	TURNING TOWARD

Begin with Against, keep going until you find your For. It's an act of defiant faith. It will give you something to lean into. It will give you a path to follow.

Choose one of your Againsts. Write an invitation for yourself to the For on its other side.

❧

Breath Prayer

Inhale: *I won't miss the rhythm of justice and healing*
Exhale: *my life can embody now.*

❧

15

Chapter 15

CHOOSE
PEACEMAKING

Are you more of a peacekeeper or a peacemaker?

What has been your own experience with conflict? How do you usually respond?

*We are always invited to be
in on what God is doing
among us and to be part of
the new way of life.*

List three invitations to peacemaking that you've experienced recently. How did you respond?

What are some of your regrets when it comes to previous invitations to peacemaking? Are there things you wish now you had done differently?

What is one way you can respond today to Jesus's invitation to participate in the healing of the world?

Write a vision for how peacemaking could be embodied in your life.

❦

Breath Prayer

Inhale: *The work that is mine to do,*
Exhale: *I will be faithful to do.*

❦

What work is yours to do right now? How can you be faithful to do it?

....

....

....

....

....

....

....

....

....

....

....

....

....

....

....

....

....

....

....

....

Learning to practice meaningful peacemaking in community has been uncomfortable and hard and also the best work I'll probably have to keep doing the rest of my life.

What are three ways that peacemaking can be embodied in your communal experience with the world around you?

———————

*Peacemaking is the simplest
hardest work we do, and every
day we show up to do it, we
repair the world just a bit more.*

———————

Create a plan for how you will respond when you fail at your ideals. What does a humble response look like for you?

Doing peacemaking work is rarely sexy and noticeable to others. How will you cultivate the habits of peacemaking in small ways in your life?

Chapter 16

YOU HAVE
PERMISSION
TO BE HAPPY

Think back over the past five to ten years. Describe your personal brand during that time.

....

....

....

....

....

....

....

....

Where did that brand come from? What were the influences and choices that shaped that brand?

....

....

....

....

....

....

....

Was there a point where your brand began to feel oppressive or restrictive to you? Who benefited from you remaining on brand?

....

....

....

....

I always thought that I would be one sort of person: but now I'm someone else.

Fill in the blanks with your own answers to these prompts. Explore the shifts and changes you've experienced in your own "brand" or life story.

I always _____ *but then* _____.

I used to _____ *but now I* _____.

I always _____ *but then* _____.

I used to _____ *but now I* _____.

I always _____ *but then* _____.

I used to _____ *but now I* _____.

I always _____ *but then* _____.

I used to _____ *but now I* _____.

Write yourself a permission slip to go off-brand.

_____ *has my permission to* _____.

Have you truly considered joy and happiness to be good motivators for transformation and faith shift?

....

....

....

....

What has been your relationship with happiness? What did your religion or faith tradition prioritize and teach and model when it came to joy?

....

....

....

....

....

....

Because the wilderness has helped us become more acquainted with grief and loss, it has also given us the pathway back toward joy and gratitude.

———————

You are allowed joy. You don't need permission to go off-brand, but in case you're looking for it, here it is: you have permission to go off-brand. . . . You have permission to experience joy and gratitude, freedom and wholeness. You have permission to be happy.

———————

Create a plan for the practice of joy in your life.

Write ten things you're grateful for today.

----

*You don't need to apologize for
the ways you're waking up to
God's good love and wide
embrace.*

What are some hobbies you enjoy for fun?

Have fun on purpose.

Is there anything you'd like to try just for the fun of it?

What are five ways you can plan to have fun on purpose?

Describe a connected communal experience you've had—it can be within a religious context or not. How did you feel in your body?

———

Right here, in your wilderness,
you have an invitation to wild,
off-brand, out-of-order joy.

———

❧

Breath Prayer

Inhale: *Moments of joy aren't erasing reality;*
Exhale: *my joy is part of reality, too.*

❧

List ten moments of unexpected joy you've experienced lately.

What is a milestone or moment in your life that deserves celebration right now? Create a plan to honor and acknowledge that moment in a way that feels good to you.

An evolving faith is always

a remix.

Take a moment to craft your own "Yes, and" declarations. Acknowledge and name the truth and then speak what is still true.

Yes _____ *and I still belong.*

....

....

....

....

Yes _____ *and I still belong.*

....

....

....

....

Yes _____ *and I still belong.*

....

....

....

....

Yes _____ *and I still belong.*

....

....

....

....

Claim your whole story. All of your life belongs to you.

Chapter 17

NOW
WE'RE JUST
GETTING STARTED

List five moments of complicated emotion or sorrow that you hold tenderly now because of how they formed you as well.

We aren't meant to be untouched or unmoved or unchanged by living. I wouldn't trade a moment of what brought me here, not now.

This Gardener of hope sees the root of life still in you and cultivates everything that is wild and unexpected, hopeful and redemptive in you, bringing forth life you never imagined, a life that repairs the world at your feet.

What do you believe we are journeying toward out here in the wilderness? Envision your own life's destination. Where do you live? Who is with you? What does home feel like? Community? Work? What are the big ideas that you want to live into now?

If you encountered someone who has found themselves at the threshold of the wilderness, what advice would you give them? What do you wish someone had told you at the early stages of your journey?

Your life can be a sanctuary for other wanderers, they will find rest in your peace.

In the book, Sarah shares her vision of a table she'd set up in the wilderness including delicious foods, paper lanterns in the trees, and an all-are-welcome guest list. If you set up a feast in the wilderness, what would it look like? Describe your own version of that makeshift table with the misfits.

....

....

....

....

....

....

....

....

What does it mean to make your home in the love of God? What would shift within you and outside of you if you believed and lived within that reality?

....

....

....

....

....

....

....

....

....

....

....

....

As you wander through the wilderness, I pray for altars to surprise you, places where you encounter the wild goodness of the Spirit's comfort and the feathered strength of God's love.

What would you like to include from or add to the practices for an evolving faith described in *Field Notes for the Wilderness*?

What are the lessons you are learning for yourself in the wilderness? What have you learned about God?

———

I pray that you would embrace a plain, ordinary sort of healing that prioritizes rest, joy, goodness, ritual, compassion, and kindness.

———

Write a blessing for the version of you who crossed the threshold into the wilderness. Give that earlier-you the blessing you wish you had received when you entered the wilderness.

Write your own benediction of hope for the wilderness and the path ahead.

....
....
....
....
....
....
....
....
....
....
....
....
....
....
....
....

Breath Prayer

Inhale: *I know who I am,*
Exhale: *I honor who I am becoming.*

Inhale: *I am loved by God,*
Exhale: *I am right where I belong.*

May you trust in God of the wilderness, knowing that, even now, you are held in the love that holds everything.

More from
SARAH BESSEY

A Collection of
Meditations for Renewal

A
RHYTHM
of
PRAYER

Edited by SARAH BESSEY

Featuring writing by Amena Brown,
Barbara Brown Taylor, Lisa Sharon Harper, and more

CONVERGENT

Available wherever books are sold